Introduction

This book covers the fundamentals of precise raw chocolate making and outlines the following topics, techniques and principals:

❦

Tempering – explains the tempering process, various ways to temper and why tempering is a crucial part of chocolate making

❦

Chocolate moulds – the different types, how to use them, how to care for them and where to buy them

❦

Base recipes for white, "milk", dark and "pure"(using nibs) chocolate – all dairy free

❦

Sweetener chart of all sweeteners to use in raw chocolate and in what amounts

❦

How to make coloured chocolate and explanation of various decorating methods

❦

Ooosha's "Signature" Chocolate recipes

❦

Creating and using textures and aroma to create truly unique raw chocolates

❦

Troubleshooting section of FAQ's on tempering and general chocolate making

❦

Links page to help you find everything you require to get started; moulds, ingredients, equipment and inspiration

Table of Contents

CONTINUES

Foreword

NOW, lets be honest. No matter what dietary path one follows, what your cultural upbringing, age, or food beliefs may be, one thing is certain; we all love chocolate! If you are shaking your head saying, 'no way, not me', we both know that you are in total denial and are just a closet lover of all things chocolate like the majority of the population. I am the first to admit it, personally I fit within the 'majority' category and have a love affair with any recipe that boasts clean, raw chocolate on occasion.

My passion for scratch cooking runs deep. I thrive on it, and it drives me to push myself to those culinary corners that are less familiar, letting the ingredients talk me through the process of creating. There is nothing better than spending the day in my kitchen developing, or cooking a recipe that is such a staple food that we tend to purchase pre-made so often, such as home made breads, fresh pasta, and of course chocolate. There are many resources, and cookbooks out there that support this creative flow in the kitchen but very few that are bold enough, and have the experience behind them as the info in this packed ebook does when venturing into this sexy world of decadence.

Over a span of about 6 years throughout the EU, with dozens of trainings, tons of large culinary events and launching 5 plant-based restaurants throughout Europe, from Istanbul, to Munich and London, I have been able to reap the benefits first hand of Amy's skills heading up the pastry menus, or rocking out service together with our team behind the line.

The finish to any meal, especially a multi course menu is truly the finale of the experience for the diner, and for this course I would trust Amy, with her passion, and willy wonka creativity to wrap up the menu, or evening with a sweet bow and a chocolate kiss to send the diner home on a cloud of euphoria and total completion.

Amy is a force in the kitchen and her work was a massive contribution to the menus we offered at those restaurants. She is not only my favorite raw pastry chef, but also a dear friend. I continue to be amazed by the innovation she continues to share with the world in the realm of raw chocolate and pastry. Try it for yourself, and trust me, you will not be disappointed, you are in good hands and that sweet tooth of yours and dinner guests will be very grateful you dove into this book as well.

Chad Sarno
Chef. Educator. Plant Pusher.
www.chadsarno.com

A few words

THE production of raw chocolate has come a very long way in the past 10 years, it used to be that dates and cacao nibs mixed together somewhat haphazardly in the food processor was considered raw chocolate. These days, people are learning how to create raw chocolate which is just like cooked; with the shine, snap and melt-in-your-mouth feel. My journey has been to educate as many people as possible in making raw chocolate to the highest possible standard using superior quality ingredients and their limitless imagination to create uniquely presented, flavoured and packaged chocolate; to turn even the biggest skeptic into a raw chocolate lover.

My hope is that through reading this book, and applying the techniques and principles outlined, you too will be on the road to making the best raw chocolate you have ever tasted. For those of you who have been making raw chocolate for a while, the skills outlined in this book will propel you into a whole other level of raw chocolate creation and answer all the questions to problems you have had over the years. If you are new to raw chocolate making, then this book will serve as an educational resource and priceless tool on your raw chocolate journey; teaching you everything you need to know from commercial production methods to making and using coloured chocolate to achieve professional results that you can be proud of.

I see raw chocolate and desserts of any kind as a gateway food; if you can attract people to healthy eating through beautifully presented and executed desserts and chocolates then you are on the road to changing the way they view "health food" and "healthy eating". If you can open one persons mind to the possibility that exists in making healthier food choices, then you are making a huge difference in the world, maybe not all at once, but one at a time, step by step.

I am truly excited for you and the chocolate journey that lies ahead and it is a journey. Don't fool yourself into thinking that you will be a pro overnight. Becoming a master chocolate maker happens over the course of many years and through much trial and error. Enjoy the journey. Enjoy the learnings that come from discovering yourself through chocolate. Above all, have fun!

Amy Levin

A Great History

Unknown Monkeys are said to have been the bringers of wild cacao trees; by eating the fruit and spitting the seeds (cacao beans) onto the ground. Thus, planting the first seeds! In Costa Rica, Panama, Peru, and Brazil Squirrel Monkeys, Capuchins, and Spider Monkeys feed heavily on the fruit of cacao trees

1500 BC – 400 BC Olmec Indians are believed to be the first to grow cacao beans as a domestic crop

400 BC – 200 BC Archaeological evidence in Costa Rica indicates that cacao was drunk by Maya traders

600 AD Mayans migrate into northern regions of South America establishing earliest known cacao plantations in the Yucatan

200 BC – 1550 AD Mayan's raised and traded cacao as a valuable commodity. Cacao was grown both in house gardens and in plantations

1376 AD – 1520 AD Cacao beans were both a valuable commodity, and a major form of currency in the Aztec empire

1502 AD Christopher Columbus, the first outsider to drink chocolate, is said to have brought back cacao beans to King Ferdinand from his fourth visit to the New World, but they were overlooked in favour of the many other treasures he had found.

1519 AD Chocolate was first noted when Spanish explorer Hernando Cortez visited the court of Emperor Montezuma of Mexico. Montezuma is said to have drank 50 goblets of cacao beverage per day as it was believed to bring strength and power to those who drank it.

1528 AD Cortez brought chocolate back from Mexico to the royal court of King Charles V. along with the secret recipe for xocoatl (chocolate drink) Monks, hidden away in Spanish monasteries, processed the cocoa beans and kept chocolate a secret for nearly a century.

1544 AD Dominican friars took a group of Kekchi Mayan nobles to visit Prince Philip of Spain. The Mayans brought gift jars of beaten cacao, mixed and ready to drink. The Spanish began to add cane sugar and flavourings such as vanilla to their sweet cacao beverages.

1585 AD The first commercial shipment occurred when a load of beans was sent from Veracruz, Mexico to Seville. For almost 100 years, preparation of the drink remained a Spanish secret, until...

1606 AD ...it was finally introduced into Italy in by Antonio Carletti and from there into France. The beverage soon became very popular, and chocolate houses spread all over Europe.

1657 AD The first "English Chocolate House" opens in Great Britain for chocolate drinking

17th – 18th Centuries Chocolate was thought to be both nourishing and an aid to digestion. In the late 17th century, chocolate houses appeared in London, alongside already flourishing coffee houses. Coffee and chocolate houses were often the scenes of gambling, political intrigue and general dissipation.

18th Century Mixing chocolate with milk instead of water was struck upon by Sir Hans Sloane, personal physician to Queen Anne. His secret recipe, eventually sold to a London apothecary, at a later date was acquired by the Cadbury brothers.

1879 Daniel Peter and Henre Nestle introduce milk chocolate to the world.

1879 Rodolphe Lindt, the founder of Lindt Chocolates, invented the process of "Conching" which is used to refine chocolate thus enhancing it's quality.

The Essential Ingredient

Cacao in all its glorious forms

Cacao Beans

Cacao beans come from the Cacao Fruit which grows in places like The Ivory Coast, Mexico and Spain. The beans are surrounded by fruit within the pod and, when eaten out of the pod, the beans bitterness is offset by the sweetness of the surrounding fruit; natures original chocolate treat. These beans are removed from the pod and, in all cooked chocolate production, but not raw, the beans are then fermented and dried (or roasted). Both the fermentation and roasting processes bring forth the layers of flavour present in the cacao bean. Without these processes, the resulting chocolate confections will be delicious, but will not be suitable for chocolate tasting to identify it's various flavour notes.

Cacao Nibs

In raw processing techniques the beans are generally not fermented. The beans are sun dried on massive roofs and raked over throughout several days for consistent drying. Once dry, they are transported to a factory where the skins are removed by a machine called a winnower, which can be a very simple machine or, in cooked chocolate, much more complex. These nibs are then either packed as is or used by some commercial raw chocolate companies to make raw chocolate bars. The cacao skins are used in animal feed.

Cacao Liquor

Is made by grinding the beans in an industrial machine into a fine paste. During this process, the cacao will be heated unless specific raw techniques are applied to keep the machine cool, therefore keeping the processing of the beans within 42c. From here, this paste is either set and sold as is or further processed to make cacao powder. (see below) This is not an ingredient used in this book, but one I encourage you to experiment with it if you feel drawn to do so.

Cacao Powder & Butter

To make cacao powder, the press (as mentioned above) extracts 75% – 90% of the fat (cacao butter) from the chocolate liquor. The remaining cake is then ground and sifted through fine nylon, silk, or wire mesh and used to make cacao powder. In my chocolate classes, there is generally a question of the flavour notes present in differing cacao powders. These chocolate flavour notes develop when the beans are fermented and roasted. Raw chocolate powder generally does not contain these flavour notes, unless the nibs are fermented, which is uncommon in raw chocolate production.

Choices

I buy all of my cacao products from Tree Harvest, as mentioned on the Links page. I buy Ecuadorian or Peruvian butter, nibs and powder as I find them to be the most consistent in flavour and the most reasonably priced. They also carry Balinese cacao products which I, and many I have spoken to, find low quality and tasting, rather surprisingly, burnt. If you are able to choose between Criollo, Forastero and Trinitario cacao products, choose Criollo as it's the Arabica coffee bean of the cacao world; the very finest.

Melts in your mouth

The process of making commercially produced chocolate, raw or cooked, and why the texture is so different from domestically/artisan produced chocolate.

FIRST time raw chocolate tasters generally have the same issue to report; it's grainy and it doesn't melt in your mouth like cooked chocolate. Here is a short explanation both for you to understand and for you to convey to those eating your chocolate, if you wish.

The process of commercial chocolate making is the same regardless of whether you are making raw or cooked chocolate; Commercial machines can be set at low processing temperatures. In chocolate factories, a conching machine is used to first process the chocolate. This machine differs depending on how simple or advanced it is, but the premiss remains the same; to grind the chocolate for long periods of time in order to achieve as smooth a consistency as possible.

Companies like Lindt conch their chocolate for 72 hours, the longer the chocolate is conched, the more easily it dissolves into your tongue, as the cacao particles become microscopic. For smaller companies, who only have one small conching machine, they may only conch their chocolate for 8 – 12 hours so they are able to produce more chocolate per week. This will of course yield a more "grainy" texture on the tongue. Of course, conching is not the only factor at play here, large companies use emulsifiers, milk powders and so on to make their chocolate smooth and silky.

It's also important to understand that the idea of making your chocolate from scratch (nibs, cacao butter, cacao powder, sweetener, etc…) is not very common in cooked chocolate making, specifically for at home cooks, but even for large chocolate companies. Instead, they would purchase couverture, small rounds (or in commercial terms, large blocks) of tempered chocolate, which they would melt down and use as they wish for enrobing, ganache, mould casting, etc…

Raw chocolate is not yet sold as couverture, unless you buy bars of tempered plain chocolate and use that, so we make our own and that is exactly the process which will be outlined and taught in this book. When processing chocolate at home using these techniques, you are blending it for maximum of 3 minutes – any longer than that and you would heat the chocolate above raw temperatures. That is a massive difference to 72 hours, so you can see why the texture is so very different. This is an interesting thing to remind your friends, family or customers of as well.

Mise en place

Literally translated means "putting in place"
in French, as in "set up" or "everything in place"
as defined by the Culinary Institute of America.

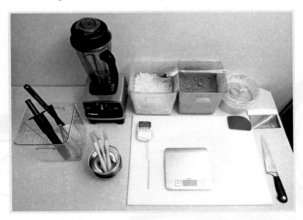

IT'S very important to begin working in a clean and tidy space. This space will set you up for the rest of your kitchen session. If you begin in a disorganized space, your work is likely to feel chaotic and frantic and the outcome could be disastrous. Set yourself up for success by preparing both mentally and physically:

1. Make sure you have ample time in the kitchen to work, uninterrupted, if possible.

2. Clean down the kitchen prior to starting work, get your work space prepared based on the goals you have for the session; chop butter, powder sugars, zest fruits, chop chocolate, temper chocolate, dry blender jug, dry utensils, clean and dry knife, set up cutting board, etc... all of this prep will allow you to work much quicker and efficiently while encouraging a calm state of mind throughout.

3. Lastly, and most important, be happy. If you are in a bad mood when you start it will only get worse and will negatively impact your final product. That is not to say that if you're not having a good day then you shouldn't work at all. It just means that if you are feeling "off" but want to go ahead, then allow more time and be gentle with yourself and the chocolate.

Tempering

Tempering refers to a process of heating and cooling chocolate
to prepare it for dipping, enrobing and casting.

The tempering process ensures that the cacao butter in
chocolate hardens in a uniform crystal structure. Chocolate that
is tempered has a smooth texture, a glossy shine and a pleasant
"snap" when bitten or broken. Chocolate that is not tempered
might be cloudy, gray, lumpy, and sticky at room temperature.
Tempering chocolate can be accomplished at home with a
chocolate, instant-read or digital thermometer, double-boiler
and/or high speed blender.

Tempering chocolate and why

Cacao butter is the fat in the cacao bean that gives chocolate its unique mouth-feel and stable properties. To be considered "real" chocolate, a chocolate bar or chunk can contain only cacao butter, not any other fat. Cacao butter is the reason why you have to "temper" real chocolate.

Cacao butter is fat that is composed of three to four glycerides of fatty acids. What complicates matters in chocolate making is that each of these different fatty acids solidifies at a different temperature. Once you melt a chocolate bar, the fatty acid crystals separate. The objective in tempering melted chocolate is to entice the fatty acid crystals of cacao butter back into one stable form.

I like to imagine that each cacao crystal is a different shape, which they kind of are, and if you try to fit all of these different shapes together there are going to be spaces in between them, which is why untempered chocolate doesn't snap and is unstable; the crystals don't fit together. When you temper the chocolate these crystals get smoothed down into one shape, let's say a square, and now all the crystals fit together so when you go to bite into or break this chocolate you will get the snap and shine we all know and love.

The temperature at which well-tempered chocolate melts is much higher than untempered chocolate because the fatty acid crystals in tempered chocolate are locked together tightly — it takes a higher temperature to pull them apart. Being tightly bound, well-tempered chocolate is resistant to developing chocolate bloom — a whitish film, streaks or spots of cacao butter that form on the surface of chocolate.

In the tempering process, melted chocolate is first cooled, causing the fatty acid crystals to form nuclei around which the other fatty acids will crystallize. Once the crystals connect, the temperature is then raised to keep them from solidifying.

Equipment needed for hand tempering

Chocolate, Digital or Candy Thermometer
(available online through Amazon)

High Speed Blender with Tamper Stick
and/or Double Boiler

Electronic Scales
(a necessity for chocolate making)

Whisks

Spatulas

Stainless Steel Mixing Bowls
(small, medium and large)

NB. Be sure all your equipment is dry before making
chocolate. To be 100% sure it's dry, put it in the
dehydrator for 5 minutes on high.

How to temper...

Tempering requires time, patience and practice.

The table top method:

This can be done either using a marble slab or table or a stainless steel table. This method is generally reserved for "pros" as you will need to work quickly and have a good "feel" for the chocolate in its fluidity and how to tell by look when it's tempered. Once your chocolate reaches 42°c, pour it out onto your work surface and, using two pastry scrapers, move the chocolate around the table until it thickens and reaches 31.5°c. This will only take a matter of minutes. Scrape tempered chocolate into a bowl and it'a ready to use. If you want it thicker, for enrobing or decorating, then keep moving it until it thickens more.

The seed method:

Seed: Is previously tempered chocolate which is shaved and added to untempered chocolate in order to assist in the tempering process. Regardless of which method you choose to temper your chocolate, seed is always a recommended addition to the tempering process.

Chocolate makers use this technique to help the chocolate to crystallize during the tempering process. The "seed" is grated tempered chocolate. It is added at the beginning of the tempering process. These crystals of tempered chocolate act like magnets, attracting the other loose crystals of fatty acids to begin the crystallization process that results in well-tempered chocolate. Of course, you will not have "seed" when you make your first batch of chocolate. This is not a problem, the chocolate will still temper without it. Once you have made your first batch, just remember to keep some "seed" tucked away in a little jar for next time.

Tempering machines:

You can often find a refurbished tempering machine on ebay for about £400 (they retail new for £1200.00) These machines can temper approx. 1.5k of chocolate at a time and are helpful if you are making chocolate as your business. The tempering machine handles all the temperature controlling for you and you don't need to be in the kitchen while it does it's work. Once it has finished tempering, the machine will hold the chocolate at 31.5°c, or whatever temperature you set it to, until you are ready to use it. Of course larger tempering machines are available, but this size is ideal for home use or you can also purchase continuous flowing table top tempering machines which start at £6,500.00 new and these process 5 Kilos of chocolate at a time, ideal for small businesses.

Standing Mixer:

Another very helpful piece of equipment which you may already own, is a standing mixer fitted with the balloon whisk. This will temper much more at a time then the tempering machine which is a time saver and most people already own a standing mixer – so a possible money saver too. The down sides of this method are that you will need to make several batches at once otherwise, the whisk will not reach the chocolate in the mixing bowl. The other issue is that because you are turning the machine on and walking away while it reduces in temperature you could easily forget it's on and the temperature could drop too low and then you have to put time into fixing this.

Be mindful of Chocolate Seize

This is when your melted chocolate mass becomes a paste that is grainy, dull, and thick. There are two conditions that bring about chocolate seize:

Water

Chocolate is made up of dry ingredients (cacao solids, "sugar" and powders) suspended in cacao butter. A small drop of liquid will moisten the dry ingredients and allow the cacao solids to clump together and separate from the cacao butter. Remember: oil and water don't mix. This is why you never cover a pot of chocolate with a lid (because the steam will condense and drop into the chocolate) and why you need to be very careful when using a double boiler. If this happens, the chocolate will not temper, but it it's not wasted; it can be used in creams, icings, ganache, spreads or truffle centres.

If this should happen, you might panic and think heat is the answer, it's not. If you add in more liquid (water, juice, milk, alcohol, etc..) to the chocolate (a minimum of 15ml of liquid per 30g of chocolate), the melted chocolate will remain in a liquid state because the dry particles get saturated by the moisture and detach from each other. They then are suspended in the liquid again so the chocolate mass is back to a liquid form. This technique is used to make chocolate sauces, syrups and frostings.

Heat

Aside from the chocolate no longer being raw, overheating separates the cacao solids and other dry ingredients from the cacao butter. Chocolate solids and dry ingredients will burn if heated to 54°c/130°f. The result is a dry, discolored paste. There's no retrieving burnt chocolate, so be very careful when heating in a double boiler or dehydrator.

Additional Fats
and the tempering process

It's nice to be able to add ingredients like nut butters, whole nuts, coconut oil and coconut manna to your chocolate for extra creaminess and depth of flavour. When tempering, there is just one rule to follow when adding any additional fats to the your chocolate base recipe.

Whether white, milk or dark chocolate, you may add an additional fat of your choice, such as macadamia nuts, coconut cream, cashews, etc… however the total amount of additional fats added to the recipe should not exceed 10% of the total weight of the recipe. This calculation should be taken from your base recipe.

For example: If the total weight of your recipe (including cacao butter, but excluding any additional fats) is 500g, you can then add 50g of an additional fat. Adding more than this will interfere with the tempering process. If you want to add more creaminess, use a plant based protein powder such as Sun Warrior or even Whey Powder as it contains very little excess fat.

Step by Step Tempering

The Vita Mix Method

Weigh out and chop or grate your cacao butter, the smaller the pieces the quicker it will melt. Now add this butter and your other solid ingredients (cashews, mulberries, vanilla bean, etc..) to the vita mix and blend on high while using the tamper stick to, persistently and quickly, push the mix into the blades.

Once the mix reaches 32°c/89°f – 35°c/95°f, a liquid state, add your powders (cacao, mesquite, lacuma/lucuma, et al) and, again using the tamper stick, push it down into the blades, working from each corner of the jug.

Every 10 seconds or so, stop and take the temperature, you don't want it to exceed 42°c/107°f (this will not harm the chocolate, but it will no longer be raw past 45°c/113°f). The higher speed you have the blender on the more heat it will produce, so towards the end, when you are going from 38° – 42°c/107°f keep it at medium – high in order to maintain control.

Once you have reached 42°c/107°f transfer your chocolate into a large mixing bowl.

If you have seed from a prior batch, you will grate it and add it at this time.

After adding the seed, whisk the chocolate until it reaches 29°c/84.2°f and then heat the chocolate back up to 31.5°c/88.7°f, either in your high speed blender or over a double boiler. In either case, be careful when doing this to not heat it above 33°c/91.4°f, if you do, you will then need to re-temper the whole batch again. As chocolate comes out of temper at 33°c/91.4°f

You now have tempered chocolate. From here you can add texture, essential oils, dried fruit, nuts etc… and pour into moulds or continue to whisk in order to reduce the temperature further to create a thicker chocolate for enrobing (dipping) or garnishing.

Step by Step Tempering

Using the Double Boiler Method

Combine all of your powder or oil based chocolate ingredients; shaved cacao butter, cacao powder, "powdered sugar" and any other powders you wish to use in a medium stainless steel or glass mixing bowl

Melt the mixture over a double boiler, being careful not to exceed 42°c/107°f, remove from the heat and whisk it very well. If you have any kind of blender, you can transfer the mix at this time and blend just to combine and get out any possible lumps in the chocolate from the powders. If you are using a vita mix to do this, you should transfer the chocolate at 37°c/98.6°f as the vita mix will conduct heat and bring the temperature to 42°c/107°f for you.

Once you have reached 42°c/107°f you need to begin reducing the temperature.

If you have seed from a prior batch, you will grate it and add it at this time.

After adding the seed, whisk the chocolate until it reaches 29°c/84.2°f and then heat the chocolate back up to 31.5°c/88.7°f, either in your high speed blender or over a double boiler. In either case, be careful when doing this to not heat it above 33°c/91.4°f, if you do, you will then need to re-temper the whole batch again. As chocolate comes out of temper at 33°c/91.4°f

You now have tempered chocolate. From here you can add texture, essential oils, dried fruit, nuts etc... and pour into moulds or continue to whisk in order to reduce the temperature further to create a thicker chocolate for enrobing (dipping) or garnishing.

Chocolate Moulds

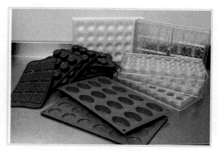

Variety of Moulds

Thermoformed/Vacuum Formed /Plastic Moulds

Thermoformed, or vacuum formed, plastic chocolate moulds are the least expensive and are intended for short production runs, craft, or hobby use. They are not very stable moulds and will warp and disfigure when washed in hot water. These are recommend for special holiday chocolates or one off events.

Silicone Rubber Moulds

Silicone rubber moulds are the second most expensive type of chocolate moulds and are very popular among artisan pastry chefs. Silicone is a type of rubber that is flexible and can handle heat, meaning it can be dried in the oven or in the dehydrator at high temperatures. I recommend Silikomart silicon moulds, as they are the most robust; others can be flimsy.

Polycarbonate Plastic Injected Moulds

Polycarbonate chocolate moulds, (sometimes referred to as european chocolate moulds, professional chocolate moulds, or confectionery grade moulds), are the most expensive type of moulds. They are usually made through the process of plastic injection mould making which involves injecting a plastic resin, usually a polycarbonate resin, around a metal master under very high pressure. These moulds have the longest life and are very strong. They are known for their ease of use and for making high gloss chocolates. This is the type of mould preferred by most professional chocolatiers and pastry chefs.

Metal Moulds

In the early days of making chocolate moulds, they were usually made out of cast metal. These moulds are not produced in quantity any more, but have retained significant value as antique and can often be found on eBay.

In the cupboard

If you don't have chocolate moulds and want to get started, you can use a lot of common kitchen items as moulds. Ice cube trays, food containers (clean and not previously used to store something strongly scented such as garlic or onion) bowls, bread or muffin tins, etc... – just bear in mind that any scratch or indentation on the "mould" will show on the chocolate. Also be sure you are using a "mould" with no indentations, as the chocolate will get stuck.

How to Use Chocolate Moulds

Using moulds to make chocolates is very simple and is the same no matter if you use plastic, silicone, or polycarbonate chocolate moulds. Just follow these simple steps:

- Make sure your chocolate moulds are clean and dry. If you are using polycarbonate moulds be sure they are at room temperature before using them and polish them with cotton wool. See "cleaning instructions" on page 6 for more information.

- Make sure there is enough room in your refrigerator to place the moulds.

- Moulds should be at room temperature when casting chocolate.

- Melt the chocolate either very gently over a double boiler being careful not to exceed 33°c or temper/re-temper your chocolate

- Fill the cavities of the mould. This can be done by using a spoon, piping bag or by pouring.

- Try not to overfill the mould as this will lead to a mess and you will have to trim the edges after you take the chocolate out of the mould. If you do overfill, run a scraper or something with a straight edge over the top of the mould to get rid of the excess chocolate.

- Once the mould is filled, lightly tap in on the counter to get rid of any air bubbles and make sure all the spaces are filled.

- Place the filled mould on a sheet pan or dehydrator tray and place in the fridge until the chocolate looks like it has hardened and separated from the mould. Tempered chocolate shrinks back from the mould.

- Once hardened, carefully remove the chocolate from the mould by placing a tray on top of the mould and then inverting it. For plastic moulds, you can flex the mould to wiggle the chocolate out, however, properly tempered chocolate will shrink when cooled and therefore fall out of the mould with ease. When using silicon moulds, you can just pop the chocolates out. For polycarbonate chocolate moulds, you should be able to just turn the mould over and the chocolate will fall out on its own, if it doesn't come out easily, be sure it's had enough time to set properly, if so, then invert it and give it some gentle taps on a table top

- If the edges of the chocolate are rough, you can clean them up by running a knife along the edge.

- Try not to touch the chocolate face too much, as it will melt and leave fingerprints. If you need to handle the chocolate during packaging, wear powder free latex gloves.

How to Clean Chocolate Moulds

It is very important to learn how to properly clean your chocolate moulds for health reasons. If chocolate residue is left on the mould, bacteria can develop and be brought into the chocolate making production cycle. Also, improper cleaning methods can destroy the mould.

Generally it is best to wash chocolate moulds in warm water with low pressure. It's ok to use detergents that are not high alkaline cleaners. Do not leave the moulds soaking in water or cleansers for a long periods of time. Do not use scrapers or razors, as any scratches they create on the moulds will appear on your chocolate. Do not put chocolate moulds in the dishwasher. Always rinse with warm water after cleansing.

Make sure to dry the chocolate moulds well, with a lint free cloth. You may also wish to shine them with a cotton ball. If you are using silicon moulds, place upside down in the dehydrator or in your oven at 100°c until they are dry (this can also be done with plastic moulds, in the dehydrator only) – do not attempt to shine silicon moulds with a cotton ball as it will leave lint on the mould. Following the mould drying step is important because water spots left in the mould can ruin the appearance of your finished chocolate.

Ask someone at your local farm shop for these handy "mushroom crates" they are great for storing your chocolate moulds.

Let the journey begin
RAW CHOCOLATE

White Chocolate

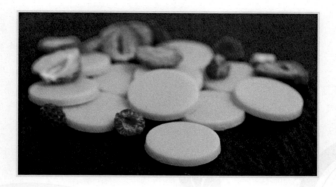

250g cacao butter – chopped or shaved with a knife

30g cashews

15g vanilla sun-warrior protein powder (optional)

See Sweetener Chart on Page 26

Pinch of crystal salt

❧ Combine all ingredients and, using the tamper stick with the blender on full high , push the ingredients down into the corners of the blender. Keep doing this until the butter is thin and the ingredients are completely smooth. This should take about 3 mins, take the temperature to be sure it's not exceeding 42°.

❧ The more you make chocolate this way, you will get used to this method and you will know when the mix is heating without needing to test it. If you are making coloured chocolate, now is the time to add the powder and blend just to combine. Transfer to a mixing bowl and follow tempering directions.

NOTE

If you are making white chocolate to use as a base for coloured chocolate, it's best to use xylitol as the sweetener as it will yield a more pure white colour than most other sweeteners. If you want to make a white chocolate for eating as is, then I recommend using a different sweetener.

Milk Chocolate

250g cacao butter _ chopped or shaved with a knife

90g cacao powder

15g vanilla sun-warrior protein powder (optional)

30g cashews

See Sweetener Chart on Page 26

Pinch crystal salt

❧ Weigh out and chop or grate your cacao butter, the smaller the pieces the quicker it will melt. Now add this butter and your other solid ingredients (cashews, mulberries, vanilla bean, etc..) to the vita mix and blend on high while using the tamper stick to, persistently and quickly, push the mix into the blades.

❧ Once the mix reaches 32°c/89°f – 35°c/95°f, a liquid state, add your powders (cacao, mesquite, lacuma/lucuma, et al) and, again using the tamper stick, push it down into the blades, working from each corner of the jug.

❧ Every 10 seconds or so, stop and take the temperature, you don't want it to exceed 42°c/107°f (this will not harm the chocolate, but it will no longer be raw past 45°c/ 113°f. The higher speed you have the blender on the more heat it will produce, so towards the end, when you are going from 38° – 42°c/107° f keep it at medium – high in order to maintain control.

❧ Once you have reached 42°c/107° f transfer your chocolate into a large mixing bowl.

❧ If you have seed from a prior batch, you will grate it and add it at this time.

❧ After adding the seed, whisk the chocolate until it reaches 29°c/84.2°f and then heat the chocolate back up to 31.5°c/88.7°f, either in your high speed blender or over a double boiler. In either case, be careful when doing this to not heat it above 33°c/91.4°f, if you do, you will then need to re-temper the whole batch again. As chocolate comes out of temper at 33°c/91.4°f

❧ You now have tempered chocolate. From here you can add texture, essential oils, dried fruit, nuts etc… and pour into moulds or continue to whisk in order to reduce the temperature further to create a thicker chocolate for enrobing (dipping) or garnishing.

Tip – if you decide not to use cashews or mulberries use the double boiler method instead of the vita mix method.

Dark Chocolate

> ❧ Combine all of your powder or oil based chocolate ingredients; shaved cacao butter, cacao powder, "powdered sugar" and any other powders you wish to use in a medium stainless steel or glass mixing bowl

> ❧ Melt the mixture over a double boiler, being careful not to exceed 42°c/107°f, remove from the heat and whisk it very well. If you have any kind of blender, you can transfer the mix at this time and blend just to combine and get out any possible lumps in the chocolate from the powders. If you are using a vita mix to do this, you should transfer the chocolate at 37c/98.6f as the vita mix will conduct heat and bring the temperature to 42°c/107°f for you.

> ❧ Once you have reached 42°c/107°f you need to begin reducing the temperature.

> ❧ If you have seed from a prior batch, you will grate it and add it at this time.

> ❧ After adding the seed, whisk the chocolate until it reaches 29°c/84.2°f and then heat the chocolate back up to 31.5°c/88.7°f, either in your high speed blender or over a double boiler. In either case, be careful when doing this to not heat it above 33°c/91.4°f, if you do, you will then need to re-temper the whole batch again. As chocolate comes out of temper at 33c/91.4f

> ❧ You now have tempered chocolate. From here you can add texture, essential oils, dried fruit, nuts etc… and pour into moulds or continue to whisk in order to reduce the temperature further to create a thicker chocolate for enrobing (dipping) or garnishing.

250g cacao butter – chopped or shaved with a knife

See Sweetener Chart on Page 26

150g cacao powder

Pinch salt

Pure Cacao Bar

For the real dark chocolate lover. This chocolate will not be as smooth as the above recipes, but is a true raw cacao bar if I have ever tasted one. Although the cacao content may not be 95% it's a very dark bar and not for the feint of heart… and certainly not for milk chocolate lovers.

250g cacao nibs

150g coconut sugar, powdered or 150 dried white mulberries

150g cacao butter

1 tsp vanilla powder

Pinch salt

➤ Combine nibs, sweetener and 50g cacao butter, using the tamper stick with the blender on full high , push the ingredients down into the corners of the blender.

➤ Keep doing this until a paste is formed and relatively smooth. This should take about 1 minute, take the temperature to be sure it's not exceeding 35°c, add the remaining cacao butter (which will help to bring the temperature down if it's gone a little too high) , vanilla and salt and blend on medium, just to melt, amalgamate and bring the temperature to 42°c.

➤ If you have seed from a prior batch, you will grate it and add it at this time.

➤ After adding the seed, whisk the chocolate until it reaches 29°c/84.2°f and then heat the chocolate back up to 31.5°c/88.7°f, either in your high speed blender or over a double boiler. In either case, be careful when doing this to not heat it above 33°c/91.4°f, if you do, you will then need to re-temper the whole batch again. As chocolate comes out of temper at 33°c/91.4°f

➤ You now have tempered chocolate. From here you can add texture, essential oils, dried fruit, nuts etc… and pour into moulds or continue to whisk in order to reduce the temperature further to create a thicker chocolate for enrobing (dipping) or garnishing.

Sweetener Chart

Use this chart as a rough guide to sweetening your various chocolates, remember these measurements are according to my taste, you may want to adjust them based on your taste or the taste of those enjoying your chocolates.

BE SURE TO READ THE NOTES AT THE BOTTOM OF THE PAGE

Sweetener	White Per 1 recipe	Milk Per 1 recipe	Dark Per 1 recipe	Pure Per 1 recipe
*Mulberries (are added whole, see * below)	100g	150g	125g – 150g	150g
Maple Sugar **NTBP	40g	75g	100g – 150g	100g
Coconut Sugar **NTBP	50g	80g	125g – 150g	125g – 150g
Xylitol **NTBP	100g	80g	100g	120g – 150g
Lacuma	50 – 50 mixed with other sweetener	50 – 50 mixed with other sweetener	50 – 50 mixed with other sweetener	50 – 50 mixed with other sweetener
Mesquite	50 – 50 mixed with other sweetener	50 – 50 mixed with other sweetener	50 – 50 mixed with other sweetener	50 – 50 mixed with other sweetener
Rapadura (has a molasses like flavour)	40g	75g	100g	100g
Raw Cane Sugar **NTBP	40g	60g	80g	80g
Banana Powder	50 – 50 mixed with other sweetener	50 – 50 mixed with other sweetener	50 – 50 mixed with other sweetener	50 – 50 mixed with other sweetener

*If using mulberries – be sure they have been dried for 48 hours in the dehydrator before using in chocolate; they must be 100% dry and crispy or they will cause the chocolate to clump. Add them at the beginning of blending, with chopped, not melted, butter to assure the optimum blending time possible.

**NTBP = needs to be powdered.
All granulated sweeteners should be made into a fine powder using a high speed blender (such as a vita mix) or a coffee grinder before using in any of the recipes in this booklet.

Cacao Content

Listing the percentage of cacao solids in your chocolate on the wrapper is a nice, professional touch. It shows that you care about your chocolate and aim to provide the highest quality. Here is a simple formula for working out the percentage of cacao solids in your chocolate, this is the same for white, milk or dark chocolate.

Butter + Mass ÷ by the total weight of the chocolate recipe

For example:

Cacao Butter – 250g

Cacao Powder – 120g

Sweetener – 100g

Total weight – 470g

Total weight of butter and mass (powder, nibs or paste) – 370g

$370 ÷ 470 = 0.787$

$0.787 × 100 = 78.7$ (rounding up) = 79%

Making your chocolates unique

and the creative process of recipe development

THERE are many ways to make your chocolates unique and to create your signature chocolate through the use of textures and aromas, you only need to open your mind and obey your creative flow!

I use the word obey because sometimes it can be very difficult for us to allow ourselves the freedom to do what we want and desire. Some of this is down to not knowing your ingredients and therefore not feeling confident with mixing and matching them in seemingly bizarre ways. However, once you work with chocolate more and allow yourself to flow into your creative process, you will begin to understand it better and it will become second nature to you. Along the way you are bound to combine things that simply do not work, accept that, take the learnings from it and move on to the next creation.

For me, the process of creating works like this:

❧ I get an idea of something I want to make and I get excited about it. I know this sounds obvious, but excitement is crucial in this process. If you are not excited – if you're stressed, hurried, pressured, unsure – you will not yield a good result.

❧ I allow this idea to marinade in my consciousness for at least a few days – I think through all the ways I can use these ingredients (dehydrated, fresh, freeze dried, as a liquid, as a solid – basically in what ever form they can be made into) which sweeteners to use (if applicable and taking into account the colour of the sweetener and how that colour will affect the final product), how these components compliment each other and how they will react to each other both in taste and in appearance.

❧ I look in recipe books or online to see if others have combined these ingredients and what their result was – what I can learn from them before I start experimenting.

❧ Finally, armed mentally with all the "research" I have done, I set forth to make this item. Sometimes, If I cannot settle on one way to proceed, I try several small batches. It must be said that sometimes you can just go for it, without pre-planning, and have real eureka moments in the kitchen! This is just my personal process, you will find yours along the way too.

Colour

Add a new dimension to your chocolates by giving them splatters, stripes or layers of colour.

In the world of cooked chocolate, coloured chocolate is made by adding colourants to cacao butter, but infusing cacao butter with colour can be a very involved process, the best way to work through that is by simply infusing the white chocolate with colour. Cacao butter lacks body as it's just an oil, however, white chocolate has body to it, given the addition of nuts, powder and/or sweetener; the colour has something to stick to and be absorbed by.

Making Coloured Chocolate

ADD the colourant at the end of blending your white chocolate, at approx. 37°c, but before tempering. To test what the colour will look like once it's cooled, before tempering, place a small amount of the coloured white chocolate on a plate and place in the freezer. The colour will really show once it's cooled and from here either add more colour or temper the chocolate to be used.

When making the coloured chocolate use a small amount of colour at a time, about ½tsp – you can always add, but you cannot take away. If you should add too much, simply supplement this by adding more white chocolate. I suggest that you either make three batches of white chocolate or split one batch of white chocolate into 3 parts and colour each one, so you have three colours on hand whenever you need them. They will last, scientifically, 1 year and practically for many months, depending on your use.

Shades of Red and Purple

Beetroot powder, red pepper powder and tomato powder

Shades of Green

Spinach powder, spirulina powder, matcha green tea powder and chlorophyll powder

Shades of Yellow and Orange

Carrot powder, turmeric powder, yellow pepper powder and ground saffron

You can easily make these powders yourself, but in most cases you will find they are not actually a powder; they have a granular texture which appears as tiny specks in your white chocolate, ruining the presentation of it. Many of these powders are available from online shops, health food stores or speciality shops like Tree Harvest. However, if you'd like to try and make these at home it's simple. Just finely slice or grate the vegetable, put on a mesh dehydrator tray and dehydrate until crisp.

Allow to cool and then, using a spice or coffee grinder or a high speed blender, blend into as fine a powder as possible. If you are using a high speed blender, you want to keep blending time to a minimum otherwise the friction of the blades against the product will create moisture and cause the powder to clump together. If this happens, put the clumped powder into the dehydrator on a teflex sheet until dry, then blend just to loosen into a powder again. Also, regardless of what piece of equipment you use, make sure it's completely dry otherwise that same problem will occur.

Decorating

First get prepared by making sure your moulds are dry and polished (if using plastic/poly moulds) and place them on top of a baking tray lined with greaseproof paper or a dehydrator tray lined with teflex.

The most effective way to learn how to work with colours, is by giving it a shot, learning how to control their temperature and what temperature you need them at for achieving different results.

The main thing to remember is that if they are more fluid, they will mix and if they are thicker, they will not. If you want to use it for brushing or splattering, it will need to be thick (lower temp 23°c – 26°c) so when it hits the mould it doesn't move. If you want to achieve a marbled or faded effect, it will need to be more fluid (higher temp 29°c – 31.5°c) so when the two colours meet, they mix easily. The more you work with colours the more confidence you will have and the more understanding you will have. Just have fun and take your time.

Splatter Effect

For this effect you will need to be working with chocolate (colour or otherwise) at a low temperature, 25 – 27°c so that it's thick enough that when it hits the mould it won't spread. Have your moulds ready and next to your bowl of chocolate. Dip a utensil of your choice into the chocolate and, while bringing the utensil up above the bowl, turn it vertically and allow ¼ of the chocolate drip off into the bowl then wiggle it quickly 4 – 6 inches above your chocolate mould creating a splatter effect. By allowing the first ¼ of the chocolate drip off into the bowl you are allowing it to come into a steady stream before placing it over the mould. Before starting on moulds you can first test this method by drizzling onto greaseproof paper or a teflex sheet just to get the hang of it. If you are using several colours on one chocolate then allow each colour to set before starting on the next.

Marbled Effect

For this effect the chocolate will need to be 29 – 31°c so they're fluid enough to mix with each other. Fill ¼ of the mould with dark, white or coloured chocolate then, from a height of about 6 inches, pour the next coloured chocolate into the mould. Once all cavities are filled place in the fridge for 20 minutes or until set.

Brushed Effect

For this effect you will need to be working with chocolate (colour or otherwise) at a low temperature, 25 – 27°c so that it's thick enough that when it hits the mould it won't spread. Using a pastry brush (the new silicon ones are not very good for this) dip into the colour you wish to use and then paint the mould as you wish. It's nice to paint the mould with white after splattering with colours as it gives a nice back round to the vibrant colours and allows them to "shine" through more. Another nice effect is using 3 colours and brushing 3 little stripes across the mould.

Layered Effect

For this effect the chocolate should be between 28 – 31.5°c and you should be using three distinctively different coloured chocolates. Fill the mould   with the first colour, allow it to set just enough that it becomes matt (is no longer shiny) and pour in the next colour and repeat the first step until the mould is full – this could be done with as little as two layers or as many as you'd like to try. As you fill the moulds layer by layer, be careful not to drip chocolate on the sides of the mould, as this will show on the finished chocolate.

Gold, Bronze and Silver Products

These come in many forms and not all of them are high quality and could be cut with other ingredients to make them less expensive. Also, not all are edible, so make sure you are buying from a good supplier. I have provided a link in the back of the book for a good supplier in the UK.

When using leaf, you must be very careful as it's incredibly delicate and light as a feather; the smallest gust of air will make it blow away. Use a paint brush or special wooden tweezers to apply leaf to the surface of chocolates or decorate the mould with the leaf and then pour chocolate into the mould. When you turn the chocolate out, the leaf will adhere to the chocolate.

Using dust or powders creates a wonderful sheen to your finished chocolates and takes it from run of the mill to extraordinary. The dusts and powders can come in a shaker jar, which is easy to use, or in a small glass jar and you would apply it using a fine paint brush.

Texture and Aroma

O N the pages to follow, you will find recipes for some of my "signature" chocolate recipes. You'll notice that each recipe has at least one texture and, in some cases, there are two different textures; soft, chewy and/or crunchy and a scent, aroma or flavour that runs throughout the entire bar so you get a burst of flavour in each bite, even if you don't get texture. When creating new flavour combinations, you want to consider the full experience for the consumer; appearance (using colour, achieving shine, packaging), aroma/smell (essential oils, flavour extracts, fresh herbs), texture (crunchy, chewy, soft, smooth) and taste (sweet, dark, bitter, floral, so on) – In most cases, chocolate you create for a child, for example, will be very different to the chocolate you create for an adult.

Using freeze dried fruit powders and pieces in your chocolate

❧ Freeze dried fruits will go soft when exposed to air, therefore it's best to mix the fruit pieces or powder into the chocolate rather than sprinkle on the surface. The only exception is if the chocolate will be sealed air tight or eaten straight away.

❧ Freeze dried fruit pieces will float in a bowl of melted chocolate because they are so light. Therefore you will need to keep mixing the chocolate in order to evenly distribute the fruit into the chocolate pieces or bars you are making

❧ An obvious note – always use as high quality freeze dried fruits as you can afford. If you can find organic, that's always the best bet when it comes to fruits. Even better, if you can find a local company that freeze dries on the premises and uses local organic fruit, you're laughing.

Using medicine flower extracts and essential oils in your chocolates

❧ Medicine flower extracts are an excellent way of adding real character and depth to your chocolate. As we discussed earlier, raw chocolate does not have the same flavour notes as cooked chocolate therefore, it's our job to create that taste journey within our chocolate for our customers, friends and family to enjoy.

❧ Essential oils are easy to find, inexpensive and there are many flavours to choose from and be inspired by. Often people ask if they are safe to use for internal consumption. All I can say is that I have used them for years and never had a problem with them. You use such a small amount per batch of chocolate that I can't see why it would cause upset. However, it's your responsibility to make that decision and to inform your customers of the ingredients being used in your bars. Always choose organic essential oil and investigate any issues that could arise from digesting them prior to using them.

Medicine Flower Extracts

Essential Oils

Using buckwheat in your chocolate

❧ Buckwheat makes a good base for transporting flavour and crunch to your chocolate without adding much flavour of it's own. However, you want to soak and very slightly sprout the buckwheat so there is only the tiniest tail formed. If you sprout it too much, it will become bitter and starchy. We are not using buckwheat for it's health properties, but rather for it's neutral, crunchy properties.

❧ Use a light sugar, such as xylitol, erythritol or raw cane sugar for flavours like lemon, orange or mint as the lightness of the "sugar" allows the key flavour to shine through.

❧ Use darker sugars, such as coconut sugar, maple sugar and rapadura for flavours like cinnamon, clove, ginger, carob and so on, the darkness of this "sugar" enhances the spices in this case and they work beautifully together.

❧ Once your buckwheat crispies (recipes to follow) are ready and cooled, store in an air tight container, preferably a glass jar, for months.

❧ The buckwheat, once mixed into chocolate, will remain crispy because the chocolate creates an air barrier and preserves it. Don't lay the buckwheat on the surface of the chocolate or it will go soft as it's exposed to the air.

Using nuts in chocolate

❧ It's best to use nuts which have been soaked, rinsed and dehydrated when adding them to chocolate. Again, we are not doing this for the health properties, but rather because when you process them in this way, they become lighter, more crisp and much more enjoyable to eat; they take on an almost roasted texture.

❧ When pouring chocolate containing nuts into the mould, use a spoon to scoop out even amount of nuts per mould. Nuts will sink to the bottom of the bowl.

❧ As mentioned above, it's best to cover the nuts completely in chocolate to avoid air getting to them and making them soft. If you are using air tight packaging when sealing your chocolates, then you should be fine. However, if they will be sitting on a platter, exposed to the air you might consider mixing in the bulk of the nuts and just scattering a couple on top for presentation.

Ooosha's Signature Chocolates

The following recipes have been perfected over many years, through much trial and error and are some of my favourite chocolate combinations of all time. Through applying the principles and techniques outlined in this book, you too will create a "signature" line over the coming years. It takes practice, patience and imagination; we all have those three traits, just need to tap into them through the muse of chocolate.

Minted Buckwheat, Lexia Raisins & Cacao Nibs in Milk Chocolate

Those who say they don't like raw chocolate, tend to love this one as it's got the classic peppermint crunch, set against non invasive milk chocolate, which appeals to first time raw chocolate tasters or children.

250g milk chocolate, melted to 31°c

8 drops peppermint essential oil

20g cacao nibs

20g lexia raisins

30g minted buckwheat

Add all ingredients to the melted chocolate and stir to evenly coat. Polish your preferred moulds and, using a spoon, evenly pour the chocolate into the room temperature moulds.

Minted Buckwheat Clusters

1c or 200g buckwheat, sprouted 12 – 24 hours (until a tail just emerges, no longer or it will be bitter)

1c or 150g xylitol, powdered

¾c packed mint, chiffonade cut

15-20 drops peppermint essential oil

Combine all ingredients in a medium mixing bowl and using your hands, mix very well. Spread the mix onto a mesh dehydrator sheet and dry for 20 hours or until completely dry. Store in an airtight jar for several months.

TIP – when drying the mixture, place a solid dehydrator sheet under it to catch any drips.

Orange Vanilla Crunch in Dark Chocolate

Orange and chocolate, a classic combination but add a crunch and you're taken into another dimension

250g milk chocolate, melted to 31°

8 drops sweet orange essential oil

3 drops vanilla medicine flower flavour extract

35g orange buckwheat crispies

Add all ingredients to the melted chocolate and stir to evenly coat. Polish your preferred moulds and, using a spoon, evenly pour the chocolate into the room temperature moulds.

Orange Buckwheat Crispies

1c or 200g buckwheat, sprouted 12 – 24 hours (until a tail just emerges, no longer or it will be bitter)

1c or 150g xylitol, powdered

30g or ¼ c fresh orange zest, using a microplane or box grater

15 drops sweet orange essential oil

½ tsp turmeric powder or yellow pepper powder (optional, for colour boost)

Combine all ingredients in a medium mixing bowl and, using your hands, mix very well. Spread the mix onto a mesh dehydrator sheet and dry for 20 hours or until completely dry. Store in an airtight jar for several months.

TIP – when drying the mixture, place a solid dehydrator sheet under it to catch any drips.

Spiced Buckwheat, Tart Cranberries & Orange in Dark Chocolate

Make this one any time of year, but it really sings around Christmas time and helps to get you in to the festive season

250g dark chocolate, melted to 31°

30g spiced buckwheat (see below)

10g freeze dried cranberries, roughly chopped

10 drops orange essential oil

½ tsp vanilla powder

Add all ingredients to the melted chocolate and stir to evenly coat. Polish your preferred moulds and, using a spoon, evenly pour the chocolate into the room temperature moulds.

Spiced Buckwheat

200g or c raw buckwheat, soaked 8 hours and sprouted 24 hours (until a tail just emerges, no longer or it will be bitter)

75g coconut sugar, powdered

2 tbsp ground cinnamon

⅛ tsp nutmeg, freshly grated

⅛ tsp ground clove

½ tsp ground mace

1 tbsp maca

⅛ tsp ground allspice

1 tsp ground cardamom

2 tsp ground ginger

Combine all ingredients in a medium mixing bowl and using your hands, mix very well. Spread the mix onto a mesh dehydrator sheet and dry for 20 hours or until completely dry. Store in an airtight jar for several months.

TIP – when drying the mixture, place a solid dehydrato sheet under it to catch any drips.

Rum Raisin Crunch in Milk Chocolate

I was never a rum & raisin kinda gal, but a former student, Barbora from Rawfully Tempting, inspired this recipe as she created something similar. This recipe is so delicious and rather moreish. Try adding the Rum Crispies to raw ice cream; divine!

250g dark chocolate, melted to 31°

30g rum crunch buckwheat

25g raisins

2 drops medicine flower rum extract

Add all ingredients to the melted chocolate and stir to evenly coat. Polish your preferred moulds and, using a spoon, evenly pour the chocolate into the room temperature moulds.

Rum Crispies

200g or 1c raw buckwheat, soaked 8 hours and sprouted 24 hours (until a tail just emerges, no longer or it will be bitter)

75g or ¾ c coconut sugar

3 drops rum medicine flower flavour extract

1 tsp cinnamon

½ tsp vanilla powder

1 tbsp maca

Combine all ingredients in a medium mixing bowl and, using your hands, mix very well. Spread the mix onto a mesh dehydrator sheet and dry for 20 hours or until completely dry. Store in an airtight jar for several months.

TIP – when drying the mixture, place a solid dehydrator sheet under it to catch any drips.

Chocolate Hemp Chia Brittle

When I was working with Chad Sarno he made a hemp seed tuille which I loved and is the inspiration behind this recipe. The Hemp Chia Brittle is delicious on it's own as much as it is smothered in dark chocolate; another brilliant addition to raw ice cream!

350 g dark chocolate

1 recipe hemp chia brittle

For this you will need a clean, dry and polished 8" x 8" square baking pan. Bring the tempered dark chocolate to 26° and pour half of it into the prepared pan, lay the sheet of hemp brittle on top and allow to cool 10 minutes or until the chocolate has slightly set. Pour remaining chocolate on top of the brittle and allow to set fully, about 20 minutes in the fridge. Once set, invert the pan onto your hand or a sheet pan, cutting board, etc… the brittle will fall out easily. Break it into large chunks and enjoy!

Alternatively, you can make these into bars by breaking the brittle into pieces that fit your mould size and using the same instructions as above.

Hemp Chia Brittle

250g hulled hemp seeds, soaked 8 hours, rinsed and drained for 5 minutes – 10 minutes to release as much liquid as possible

20g chia seed powder

30g chia seeds, soaked in 150g water for 1 hour – overnight

½ tsp vanilla powder

100g coconut nectar or maple syrup

50g coconut sugar, powdered

Pinch himalayan crystal salt

Combine all ingredients in a medium mixing bowl and mix to combine evenly. Spread ½ inch thick in a 7.5"x 7.5" square on a teflex lined dehydrator sheet and dehydrate 10 hours or until ready to flip off the teflex and transfer onto a mesh tray. Dehydrate until crisp, about 12 hours.

Starry Night

Star anise is so nice in chocolate and it's an uncommon combination, so make it for friends and family and enjoy watching them as they try to figure out the secret ingredient

250g dark chocolate, melted to 31°

50g star anise candied hazelnuts, crushed with mortar & pestle into a rough crumble consistency

8 drops star anise or sweet fennel essential oil

100g white chocolate, melted to 30°

Fill your moulds with white and allow to set, about 15 minutes at room temperature. Meanwhile, in a mixing bowl combine dark chocolate, star anise candied hazelnuts and essential oil and mix to combine. Once the white chocolate is matt (no longer shiny, but not fully set) , fill the rest of the mould with the dark chocolate. The nuts will likely sink to the bottom, so be sure to spoon some out into each mould evenly.

Star Anise Candied Hazelnuts

200g hazelnuts, soaked 8 hours – overnight, rinsed and drained

75g coconut sugar, powdered

2 tbsp maple syrup

½ tsp crystal salt

2 tsp ground anise seed

8 drops star anise essential oil

In a food processor blend all ingredients until the nuts have slightly broken down into a large crumble texture. Transfer the mix to a teflex lined dehydrator tray and spread into an even layer. Dehydrate 10 hours, flip onto a mesh sheet, dry further 10 hours or until dry and crisp. Break into small pieces and store in an airtight container until ready to use.

Cherry & Almond in Milk Chocolate

A classic combination and for good reason! The Cherry and Almond Medicine Flower Extracts mean that you get that wonderful marriage of flavour in every bite and by soaking and dehydrating the almonds, you create a "roasted" almond texture to accompany the sweet crunch of freeze dried cherry.

250g milk chocolate, melted to 31°

40g almonds, soaked 8 hours, rinsed and dehydrated till crispy

15g freeze dried sweet or sour cherries

5 drops black cherry medicine flower extract

5 drops almond medicine flower extract

Press the almonds between your thump and first finger so they break in half down the middle. Add all ingredients to the melted chocolate and stir to evenly coat. Polish your preferred moulds and, using a spoon, evenly pour the chocolate into the room temperature moulds.

Warm Embrace

The warmth of cinnamon and maca play against the earthiness of almond and sticky apricot to bring you comfort on the coldest of nights

250g dark chocolate, melted to 31°c

20g dried, un-sulphured apricots, roughly chopped

2 tsp maca powder

1 tsp ground cinnamon

25g almonds, soaked, rinsed, dehydrated and roughly chopped

1½ tsp almond extract

Place apricots in a medium bowl and mix in the maca and cinnamon powder to coat all the apricot pieces, this will prevent them from sticking together. Add the remaining ingredients and stir to combine. Pour into your prepared moulds. The fruit and nuts will likely sink to the bottom, so be sure to spoon some out into each mould evenly.

Cheeky Monkey

A wonderful balance of texture and aroma create a taste
sensation in this playful yet sophisticated chocolate

250g milk chocolate, melted to 31°c

20g desiccated or shredded coconut

30g dried white mulberries

30g pecans, soaked 4 hours, rinsed and
dehydrated

10g banana powder

5 drops medicine flower banana extract

10 – 15 drops medicine flower coffee extract

Combine all ingredients in a medium mixing bowl and
mix to evenly coat. Pour into your prepared mould of
choice, bar moulds or bark works best for this
chocolate.

Breakfast Bark

I wish my mom packed these into my bagged lunch when I was a kid... or now.

250g dark chocolate

2 tbsp or 15g chia seeds

¼ c or 20g goji berries

30g raw rolled oats

1 tbsp or 15g bee pollen

25g almonds, soaked, rinsed and dehydrated

2 tsp reishi mushroom powder

1 tbsp or 10g sun warrior protein powder, or your favourite protein powder

1 tbsp or 10g lacuma

½ tsp vanilla powder

Bring chocolate to 28°c. Add all ingredients to your chocolate and pour onto a teflex lined dehydrator tray or onto a greaseproof paper lined baking tray. Alternatively, pour into a mould of your choice. Place in the fridge to set, about 25 minutes. Break into pieces and store in a glass jar.

Chipotle Candied Macadamias in Dark Chocolate

Warm, comforting and smokey with a tart hit of lime in the macadamias; a brilliant combination

250g milk chocolate

30g chipotle candied macadamia nuts, roughly chopped

Polish your moulds (if using professional or plastic moulds) with cotton wool. Bring chocolate to 31°c and mix in all other ingredients to combine. Pour into your prepared mould of choice, being sure to scoop some of those lovely macadamias into each cavity evenly.

Chipotle Candied Macadamias

200g macadamias, soaked 4 hours or overnigh

2 tsp chiptole chili powder

50ml lime juice, approx 3 limes

1 tsp tamari

100g coconut sugar

1 tbsp lime zest, approx 4 limes, using a microplane or box grater

In a food processor fitted with the "S" blade, chop the macadamias into a rough crumble consistency. Transfe to a mixing bowl and add remaining ingredients, mix well to combine. Spread onto a solid dehydrator tray and dehydrate 12 hours on 115, flip onto mesh, break the clumps apart and dehydrate further 10 –12 hours or until dry. Allow to cool before using in chocolate recipe. Store in an airtight jar for months.

TIP – don't be tempted by lime essential oil or lime powder, they do not have a true lime flavour but instead are rather artificial tasting. Stick with the real stuff until Medicine Flower bring out a lime flavour extract.

Earl Grey, Raspberry & Lemon in Milk Chocolate

This is such a gorgeous chocolate, it's floral, tart, sweet, fruity… perfection!

250g Cacao Butter

70g Cacao powder

15g Sun Warrior Protein Powder

115g Coconut Sugar

20g earl grey tea leaves, powdered in spice mill

20g freeze dried raspberry powder

3 drops bergamont essential oil

10 drops lemon essential oil

5 drops medicine flower raspberry extract

❧ Melt the cacao butter in a double boiler, remove from heat, add the tea powder and allow to steep 15 minutes – 1 hour. Place back on the heat, if needed, to bring back liquid, but not exceeding 37°c.

❧ Add the cacao powder, protein powder and coconut sugar to the bowl, whisk to combine and pour into vita mix.

❧ Blend on high until the temperature reaches 42°c, this will only take about 3 – 5 seconds.

❧ Once you have reached 42°c/107°f transfer your chocolate into a large mixing bowl.

❧ If you have dark or milk seed from a prior batch, grate it and add it at this time.

❧ After adding the seed, whisk the chocolate until it reaches 29°c/84.2°f and then heat the chocolate back up to 31.5°c/88.7°f, either in your high speed blender or over a double boiler. In either case, be careful when doing this to not heat it above 33°c/91.4°f, if you do, you will then need to re-temper the whole batch again. As chocolate comes out of temper at 33°c/91.4°f

❧ You now have tempered chocolate. From here you can add texture, essential oils, dried fruit, nuts etc… and pour into moulds or continue to whisk in order to reduce the temperature further to create a thicker chocolate for enrobing (dipping) or garnishing.

Troubleshooting

Why are there streaks in my chocolate?

This is generally due to uneven tempering, meaning that the chocolate around the edges of the bowl tempered first and then mixed into the untempered chocolate. This can happen if you are in a cold room and allow the chocolate to sit for more than a minute or so during the tempering process. If you want to speed up tempering by stirring the chocolate in a cold place, you must gently stir and scrape the sides of the bowl with a spatula consistently until it's tempered.

Why is the face of my chocolate shiny, but the back is dull?

The chocolate becomes shiny because it's pressed against a clean and polished surface, like a mould or a piece of foil. The back of your chocolate is not being pressed against anything, so it won't be shiny. If you want it to be shiny, you can fill the moulds, lay a piece of acetate over the back and seal down using a pastry scraper/ dough scraper. Set the chocolate like this and then simply peel off the acetate once the chocolate is set.

Why won't my chocolate come out of the polycarbonate mould?

If your chocolate is not setting properly it's likely that you have not tempered it properly. To get the chocolate out of the mould, place it in the freezer for 15 minutes. This will force the chocolate to contract (which it normally does when it's properly tempered) so that you can easily release it from the mould by inverting it. Next, trace your steps to see where you might have gone wrong.

I got a little water in my chocolate. How can I fix it?

Unfortunately, there is no fixing that. If it's a very little bit, like a drop or two, you might get away with it, but anything more than that is not fixable. The chocolate is not totally ruined though, it can be used to make chocolate sauce by simply adding more liquid, about 1 tbsp at a time until it's chocolate sauce consistency.

How do I make a nut free white chocolate?

If you are not using nuts, then you simply need more solids in the recipe in order to make it a thicker, chocolate like consistency. Either use more sun – warrior powder, whey powder or lacuma. If you use lacuma, you will not achieve a pure white colour and therefor couldn't use it as a base for making coloured chocolate.

Can I use whey protein powder in my chocolate?

Absolutely! It's delicious and low fat, which means you can use quiet a bit of it to get a nice creamy flavour and mouth feel without adding too much fat and making it un-temperable.

Can I use coconut oil or cream in my chocolate?

You sure can, just make sure that it doesn't exceed 10% of the total weight of the recipe (see page 18) as coconut products do not temper and adding too much will inhibit the chocolates ability to temper. This same rule applies to nuts and nut butters. Is it necessary, when tempering, to bring the temperature to 42 then to 29 and back up to 31.5, as I have read that it's not necessary. When I temper, I go to 42c then down to 31.5c and that's all, I don't reheat. I have been making chocolate this way for years without any tempering issues. Much of what you will find on the internet is that bringing it to 29c and then back up to 31.5 is a necessary step and completes the tempering process. I would say go with what you want to do in this situation.

My vita mix seems to burn out when making chocolate in the way you have outlined. Why?

Try melting the cacao slightly to lubricate the vita mix and make start up easier. Also, try warming the vita mix jug in the dehydrator so the butter melts quicker. Finally, make sure you are using the tamper stick to keep things moving during the first 30 seconds of blending and that the machine is on the higest setting. If you are making chocolate which doesn't require intense processing (if you are not using nuts, mulberries, vanilla pod, etc) then you can melt the whole mix (cacao butter, cacao powder and powdered sweetener) 70% over a double boiler, whisk to combine and then use the blender just to smooth the powders out, make sure the consistency is even and bring the temperature to 42c.

Can I put my chocolate moulds through the dishwasher?

You can, but it's not recommended. It's best to wash them by hand with very hot water and eco friendly soap (harsh soaps can cause damage to your moulds) also, putting them in the dishwasher can leave a film on them which will show on your chocolates.

Why do I need to powder coconut sugar and xylitol?

Won't they just melt into the chocolate while blending? This is a common assumption, but no, they will not melt down. You need to powder all sweeteners or ingredients that are not considered a flour consistency. The only exception to this is if you are using a melanger / stone grinder which will grind the mixture to a fine paste over 12 – 72 hours.

Will you be able to taste the colourant (spirulina, tumeric or beetroot powder) when using it to colour white chocolate?

If you eat the chocolate as is, then probably, but if you use it only to decorate then no. You should only be using enough to add colour to the face of the chocolate, not so that it runs throughout the chocolate.

I live in a humid environment, can I still temper chocolate?

Yes, you can, it will just take some preparation. The room temperature should not exceed 18°c – 20°c/65°f – 70°f and relative humidity should not exceed 50% (although I have gotten away with 60%). You will need make sure that you close all windows and doors for at least 3 days prior to making chocolate and have your air conditioner set to 20°c/70°f for at least 2 days prior to making chocolate; this will remove the moisture from the air. Once you have tempered all your chocolate, store it in the fridge in an airtight container. When you want to eat it or use it, remove from the fridge about 1 hour prior to needing it. Allow it to sit at room temperature for 1 hour, this will allow it time to acclimate to the temperature change between the fridge and the room temperature. After 1 hour, or more, you can remove the lid and use the chocolate. You can also try storing it at room temperature, in a sealed container, as long as you have the A/C on and no windows opened for prolong times; it may not work so do a trial first.

Storing and using previously tempered chocolate

❧ Once a batch of basic chocolate has been made and tempered, it will keep up to 1 year under the right conditions (cool, dry environment and in an air sealed container)

❧ This chocolate can be melted down and re-tempered time and time again. The most important thing to understand is, when melting down previously tempered chocolate, you must keep the temperature below 33°c otherwise, you'll need to temper it all over again. This can be a little tricky, my suggestion is that you melt the chocolate down completely and re-temper so you know it's going to be perfect. If you want to try melting it and not exceeding 33°c then you will want to do this over a double boiler. Bring a small amount of water to the boil and reduce the temperature to a gentle simmer, place your bowl of grated or shaved chocolate on top and allow to melt completely, this takes about 1 hour depending on the room temperature. This is why I recommend tempering it again, it's just more safe, predictable and, in most cases, faster.

❧ If you are using different sweeteners on different batches of chocolate, then you will want to store these separate from one another.

❧ Some of the recipes in this book will call for the chocolate to be at a certain temperature, for example 25°c – 27°c , this is because when chocolate cools it becomes thicker. There are some cases where this is what you want, for example when enrobing or making chocolate nut clusters, and there are some cases where you want it at 31°c – this is for making basic chocolate with only the addition of dry ingredients being cast into moulds.

Caring for your chocolate

You dedicate so much time and love into making your chocolates, but the care doesn't stop there. Chocolate needs a good living environment in order to stay fresh and as delicious as the day you made it.

❧ Store in an airtight container at room temperature for 6 months – 1 year (if you are making chocolate commercially then you will want to get them scientifically tested for shelf life)

❧ If the room is over 20c/68f then the chocolates should be stored in an airtight container in the fridge for no more than 2 weeks. This time frame is dependent on the temp of your fridge and the external temp of the room. For example, if the fridge is 5c/41f and the external temp is 30c/85f with humidity then when you remove the chocolates from the fridge you will get condensation forming on the chocolates which will ruin their appearance, as this is introducing water to chocolate, and their texture will be grainy and waxy. If you are able to, set your fridge to 10c/50f so that when you remove the chocolates, they will not get so much of a shock. Most domestic fridges will be set to this temp anyway, but if you are working with a commercial fridge the temps are required to be much lower.

❧ Be sure when storing them that they are air sealed and away from other strong smelling foods such as garlic and onions as chocolate easily takes on the flavour of what's around it.

❧ If you have used fresh ingredients in your chocolates such as berries or filled them with jam, then they are best consumed on the same day. However, they will keep for 2 – 3 days in the fridge.

Nutrition and Chocolate

Today, our knowledge of the beneficial physiological actions of phytochemicals (plant chemicals) is still not fully understood but continues to grow every year with regards to preventative health mechanisms in the body. We are slowly revealing and discovering that these phytochemicals gently manipulate positive effects on our health in many significant ways.

Phytochemicals are chemical substances found in various plant foods that have specific expression and activity on many bodily functions. They are metabolites, produced by the plant in response to a hostile environment; weather, attack from pests, animals etc. The plant uses these chemicals to protect itself, and when we consume those plants, we use them to protect us.

One group of phytochemicals, flavonoids, rank amongst the most health-protective micronutrients yet discovered[1]. Chocolate contains numerous substances, but the most interesting, with regards to our health, are these flavonoids, found in abundance in the form of epicatechins[2]. It was in 1999 that chocolate was examined for catechins and dark chocolate was found to contain 53.5mg/100mg[3].

Flavonoids are absorbed in the small intestine, where they are metabolised to create compounds that positively affect numerous cell signalling pathways in the body. The end affect, is protection from disease. They stimulate a part of our detoxification system that binds to toxicants to take them out of our bodies. They inhibit tumour invasion[4], which simply means they reduce the growth of tumours in the body and most importantly, they decrease inflammation which is the underlying cause of most sickness and disease.

Chocolate consumption itself has been linked to numerous health studies related to disease:

Anti-inflammatory – inflammation is a key component in all chronic disease. The anti-inflammatory benefit was discovered by scientists researching the Kuna Indians, a tribe who originally lived on islands near Panama. They drank, on average, 5 cups of homemade, unprocessed, flavonol-rich cocoa every day. Part of their tribe migrated to Panama City and stopped this traditional consumption. Kunas living on the mainland started to develop higher blood pressure and kidney malfunction. They also experienced significantly higher risks of heart disease and cancer. In fact, the risk of death from cancer was a staggering 630% higher than the Kunas still living on the islands and consuming their cocoa drink[5].

Blood pressure lowering – a study following 470 Dutch men with an average age of 72 were followed for 15 years to measure the impact of cocoa in their diet[6]. The results showed a 50% reduction in all cause mortality and those who consumed more cocoa had lower blood pressure.[7] Chocolate helps to dilate blood vessels at around 45-100g a day[8].

Heart protective – Chocolate's cardio protective agents have not only been shown in reducing blood pressure but also increasing levels of healthy forms of cholesterol (HDL).[9]

Brain beneficial – The substances in chocolate have been linked to beneficial improvement in the regions of the brain involving learning and memory. They provoke neurogenesis, which is the stimulation of new neurons (brain cells)[10] and they protect neurons from injury.

Anxiety reliever – There is strong evidence suggesting that daily consumption of 40 g of dark chocolate during a period of 2 weeks is sufficient to reduce anxiety[11].

Cancer protective – In 2002, a special cancer facility in Strasbourg found that the flavonols in chocolate effectively inhibited the growth of colon cancer cells[12]. University of Barcelona researchers then published the first paper which began to reveal how chocolate was doing this, by switching on and off a number of pro- and anti-cell growth genes in the cancer cells.[13]

Positive mood – Chocolate induces positive effects on mood[14], but if you're reading this book, it's unlikely you'll need convincing of that!

The evidence is there, that chocolate is a health food. In spite of its perceived negative image within the general public with respect to obesity, tooth decay, acne and migraine, the scientific evidence is that chocolate does not play a significant role in any of these, provided it is eaten in normal amounts as part of a balanced diet.[15]

Absorption is a factor to consider, and flavonoid content will be hindered by[16]:

➤ Agricultural practices

➤ Ripening (more flavonoids in ripe foods)

➤ Processing (the less processed the more flavonoids)

➤ Storing (the longer you store foods the less flavonoids it contains)

➤ Cooking (some flavonoids are destroyed by heat)

In a world where "convenience" has become priority, we have put our trust in food manufacturers to supply our "nutrition". Unfortunately, this has been abused in favour of providing cheap alternatives that leave us with food that is far removed from nature and it's nutritionally-rich, chemical minefield. Raw chocolate can not only put back some key missing phytochemicals, but from Amy's recipes, put a big chocolate smile on your face and whoever else who tries your chocolate creations.

Emma Mihill
Naturopath, Nutritional Therapist, Iridologist
ND, NT Dip CNM, BA Hons, MGNI, mBANT

www.emmamihill.com
www.perfect-chocolate.co.uk

Nutrition References

[1] Knekt P et al., Am J Clin Nut 76:560-568, 2002

[2] Nehlig, A. (2013). The neuroprotective effects of cocoa flavanol and its influence on cognitive performance. *British Journal of Clinical Pharmacology*, 75(3), 716-727.

[3] S.T. Beckett, *Industrial Chocolate Manufacture and Use*, Blackwell, Oxford, UK. 1999

[4] 49 Phytochemicals in Human Health (Williams et al 2004; Kong et al 2001; Bagli et al 2004; O'Leary et al 2004)

[5] Mao TK, Powell J, Van de Water J, et al. The effect of cocoa procyanidins on the transcription and secretion of interleukin 1beta in peripheral blood mononuclear cells. *Life Sci*. 2000; 66:1377-1386. Mao TK, Powell JJ, Van de Water J, et al. The influence of cocoa procyanidins on the transcription of interleukin-2 in peripheral blood mononuclear cells. *Int J Immunotherapy* 1999; 15:23-29.

N, Sakane T. Polyphenols in chocolate, which have antioxidant activity, modulate immune function in humans in vitro. *Cell Immunol*. 1997; 177:129-136.

[6] uijsse B, Feskens EJ, Kok FJ, Kromhout D. Cocoa intake, blood pressure, and cardiovascular mortality: the Zutphen Elderly Study. *Arch Intern Med*. 2006 Feb 27;166(4):411-7

[7] Fisher NDL and Hollenberg NK. Flavanols for cardiovascular health: The science behind the sweetness. *Journal of Hypertension* 2005 August;23:1453-1459

[8] (Duffy et al 2001; Hodgson et al 2002; Stein et al 1999; Engler et al 2004; Wang-Polagruto et al 2006)

[9] Mursu J, Voutilainen S, Nurmi T, Rissanen TH, Virtanen JK, Kaikkonen J, Nyyssonen K, Salonen JT. Dark Chocolate Consumption Increases HDL Cholesterol Concentration and Chocolate Fatty Acids May Inhibit Lipid Peroxidation in Healthy Humans. *Free Radic Biol Med*. 2004 Nov 1;37(9):1351-9.

[10] Nehlig, A. (2013). The neuroprotective effects of cocoa flavanol and its influence on cognitive performance. *British Journal of Clinical Pharmacology*, 75(3), 716-727.

[11] Martin et al. Metabolic Effects of Dark Chocolate Consumption on Energy, Gut Microbiota, and Stress-Related Metabolism in Free-Living Subjects. *Journal of Proteome Research*, 2009; 091007113151065

[12] Carnesecchi S, Schneider Y, Lazarus SA, Coehlo D, Gosse F, Raul F. Flavanols and procyanidins of cocoa and chocolate inhibit growth and polyamine biosynthesis of human colonic cancer cells. *Cancer Lett*. 2002 Jan 25;175(2):147-55

[13] Noe V, Penuelas S, Lamuela-Raventos RM, Permanyer J, Ciudad CJ, Izquierdo-Pulido M. Epicatechin and a cocoa polyphenolic extract modulate gene expression in human Caco-2 cells. *J Nutr*. 2004 Oct;134(10):2509-16

[14] Nehlig, A. (2013). The neuroprotective effects of cocoa flavanol and its influence on cognitive performance. *British Journal of Clinical Pharmacology*, 75(3), 716-727

[15] Beckett, S.T, *Science of Chocolate*, 2nd edition, Royal Society of Chemistry, Feb 2008.

[16] Mattson MP. Dietary factors, hormesis and health. *Ageing Res Rev*. 2008;7(1):43-48

Tools & Ingredients

Instead of making a long list here of all the products and pieces of equipment and where to buy them, I have created a comprehensive list of everything you will need and put it on my website. As much as possible, I have added buying options has buying options for the USA and the UK/Europe.

Visit ooosha.co.uk
and look under Tools & Ingredients

Amy Levin

Amy is a classically trained professional chef who found her way into vegan and vegetarian raw food in 2004 while training to be a holistic health counselor at The Institute of Integrative Nutrition.

After working for several of the UK's most respected raw food & chocolate companies, Amy was able to apply that new found talent and knowledge to her role as Senior Sous and Pastry Chef to World Renowned Executive Chef, Chad Sarno at Saf London & Munich during their opening years.

Amy currently teaches various raw chocolate and raw food classes from her home in South London, and throughout the UK and North America. She consults with businesses who wish to implement only the very best raw chocolates and desserts into their menu or product line. Her highly sought after live Fundamentals and Advanced Raw Chocolate making classes have now been made into online learning courses and additional raw confectionary based courses will follow shortly.

"Amy Levin is, by far, one of the leading chocolatiers on the modern food scene today. Amy was one of the first Chefs to finally figure out, adapt and then cleverly employ classical chocolate making techniques in the realm of healthy vegan chocolate. This seemingly simple adaptation was at once elementary and revolutionary and sorely needed in the healthy food movement.

Gone now is the excuse: 'well this chocolate melts in your hands because it's vegan'! Amy's amazing book is perfect for established Chefs as well as the beginner. You will be delighted with the information in the book, the style in which it is written and most importantly the delectable products which you will produce!"

Chef Peter Cervoni

Ooosha

Notes

Notes

Notes

Made in the USA
San Bernardino, CA
24 September 2015